HAL•LEONARD

INSTRUMENTAL PLAY-ALONG

TROMBONE

AUDIO
ACCESS
INCLUDED

PLAYBACK+
Speed • Pitch • Balance • Loop

HIT SONGS

T0070321

Audio arrangements by Peter Deneff

To access audio, visit:
www.halleonard.com/mylibrary

Enter Code
4610-3086-1120-6876

ISBN 978-1-70515-014-6

HAL•LEONARD®

For all works contained herein:
Unauthorized copying, arranging, adapting, recording, Internet posting, public performance,
or other distribution of the music in this publication is an infringement of copyright.
Infringers are liable under the law.

Visit Hal Leonard Online at
www.halleonard.com

Contact us:
Hal Leonard
7777 West Bluemound Road
Milwaukee, WI 53213
Email: info@halleonard.com

In Europe, contact:
Hal Leonard Europe Limited
42 Wigmore Street
Marylebone, London, W1U 2RN
Email: info@halleonardeurope.com

In Australia, contact:
Hal Leonard Australia Pty. Ltd.
4 Lentara Court
Cheltenham, Victoria, 3192 Australia
Email: info@halleonard.com.au

CONTENTS

ADORE YOU

TROMBONE

Words and Music by HARRY STYLES,
THOMAS HULL, TYLER JOHNSON
and AMY ALLEN

Copyright © 2019 HSA PUBLISHING LTD., UNIVERSAL MUSIC PUBLISHING LTD., THESE ARE PULSE SONGS, ONE YEAR YESTERDAY PUBLISHING,
CREATIVE PULSE MUSIC, SNAPPED BACK SONGS, KENNY + BETTY TUNES and ARTIST PUBLISHING GROUP WEST
All Rights for HSA PUBLISHING LTD. Administered by UNIVERSAL MUSIC WORKS
All Rights for UNIVERSAL MUSIC PUBLISHING LTD. Administered by UNIVERSAL - POLYGRAM INTERNATIONAL PUBLISHING, INC.
All Rights for THESE ARE PULSE SONGS, ONE YEAR YESTERDAY PUBLISHING and CREATIVE PULSE MUSIC
Administered by CONCORD COPYRIGHTS c/o CONCORD MUSIC PUBLISHING
All Rights for SNAPPED BACK SONGS, KENNY + BETTY TUNES and ARTIST PUBLISHING GROUP WEST
Administered Worldwide by KOBALT SONGS MUSIC PUBLISHING
All Rights Reserved   Used by Permission

ANYONE

TROMBONE

Words and Music by JUSTIN BIEBER,
JON BELLION, JORDAN JOHNSON,
ALEXANDER IZQUIERDO, ANDREW WATT,
RAUL CUBINA, STEFAN JOHNSON
and MICHAEL POLLACK

Copyright © 2020 UNIVERSAL MUSIC CORP., BIEBER TIME PUBLISHING, SONGS OF UNIVERSAL, INC., ART IN THE FODDER MUSIC,
BMG BUMBLEBEE, SONGS OF A BEAUTIFUL MIND, BMG PLATINUM SONGS US, SONGS OF BBMG, BMG GOLD SONGS, AIX MUSIC PUBLISHING,
ANDREW WATT MUSIC, RIC VOLTA PUBLISHING, KMR MUSIC ROYALTIES II SCSP, 1916 PUBLISHING,
WARNER-TAMERLANE PUBLISHING CORP., WHAT KEY DO YOU WANT IT IN MUSIC and SONGS WITH A PURE TONE
All Rights for BIEBER TIME PUBLISHING Administered by UNIVERSAL MUSIC CORP.
All Rights for ART IN THE FODDER MUSIC Administered by SONGS OF UNIVERSAL, INC.
All Rights for BMG BUMBLEBEE, SONGS OF A BEAUTIFUL MIND, BMG PLATINUM SONGS US, SONGS OF BBMG, BMG GOLD SONGS
and AIX MUSIC PUBLISHING Administered by BMG RIGHTS MANAGEMENT (US) LLC
All Rights for ANDREW WATT MUSIC, RIC VOLTA PUBLISHING and KMR MUSIC ROYALTIES II SCSP
Administered Worldwide by SONGS OF KOBALT MUSIC PUBLISHING
All Rights for 1916 PUBLISHING Administered Worldwide by KOBALT SONGS MUSIC PUBLISHING
All Rights for WHAT KEY DO YOU WANT IT IN MUSIC and SONGS WITH A PURE TONE Administered by WARNER-TAMERLANE PUBLISHING CORP.
All Rights Reserved   Used by Permission

BAD HABITS

TROMBONE

Words and Music by ED SHEERAN,
JOHNNY McDAID and FRED GIBSON

Copyright © 2021 Sony Music Publishing (UK) Limited, Spirit B-Unique Polar Patrol and Promised Land Music Ltd.
All Rights on behalf of Sony Music Publishing (UK) Limited Administered by Sony Music Publishing LLC, 424 Church Street, Suite 1200, Nashville, TN 37219
All Rights on behalf of Spirit B-Unique Polar Patrol Administered by Spirit B-Unique Polar Patrol Songs
All Rights on behalf of Promised Land Music Ltd. Administered by Universal Music Works
International Copyright Secured   All Rights Reserved

BANG!

TROMBONE

Words and Music by ADAM METZGER,
JACK METZGER and RYAN METZGER

Copyright © 2020 AMAB Songs
All Rights Administered Worldwide by Songs Of Kobalt Music Publishing
All Rights Reserved   Used by Permission

BLINDING LIGHTS

TROMBONE

Words and Music by ABEL TESFAYE,
MAX MARTIN, JASON QUENNEVILLE,
OSCAR HOLTER and AHMAD BALSHE

Moderately

Copyright © 2019 KMR Music Royalties II SCSp, MXM, Universal Music Corp., Sal And Co LP, WC Music Corp. and Wolf Cousins
All Rights for KMR Music Royalties II SCSp and MXM Administered Worldwide by Kobalt Songs Music Publishing
All Rights for Sal And Co LP Administered by Universal Music Corp.
All Rights for Wolf Cousins Administered by WC Music Corp.
All Rights Reserved   Used by Permission

CIRCLES

TROMBONE

Words and Music by AUSTIN POST,
KAAN GUNESBERK, LOUIS BELL,
WILLIAM WALSH and ADAM FEENEY

Moderately

Copyright © 2019 SONGS OF UNIVERSAL, INC., POSTY PUBLISHING, UNIVERSAL MUSIC CORP.,
EMI APRIL MUSIC INC., NYANKINGMUSIC, WMMW PUBLISHING and QUIET AS KEPT MUSIC INC.
All Rights for POSTY PUBLISHING Administered by SONGS OF UNIVERSAL, INC.
All Rights for EMI APRIL MUSIC INC., NYANKINGMUSIC, WMMW PUBLISHING and QUIET AS KEPT MUSIC INC.
Administered by SONY MUSIC PUBLISHING LLC, 424 Church Street, Suite 1200, Nashville, TN 37219
All Rights Reserved   Used by Permission

DRIVERS LICENSE

TROMBONE

Words and Music by OLIVIA RODRIGO
and DANIEL NIGRO

Copyright © 2021 Sony Music Publishing LLC, Liv Laf Luv and Daniel Leonard Nigro Music
All Rights Administered by Sony Music Publishing LLC, 424 Church Street, Suite 1200, Nashville, TN 37219
International Copyright Secured   All Rights Reserved

HEATHER

TROMBONE

Words and Music by
CONAN GRAY

Moderately

Copyright © 2020 Sony Music Publishing LLC
All Rights Administered by Sony Music Publishing LLC, 424 Church Street, Suite 1200, Nashville, TN 37219
International Copyright Secured   All Rights Reserved

THEREFORE I AM

TROMBONE

Words and Music by BILLIE EILISH O'CONNELL
and FINNEAS O'CONNELL

Copyright © 2020 UNIVERSAL MUSIC CORP., DRUP and LAST FRONTIER
All Rights for DRUP Administered by UNIVERSAL MUSIC CORP.
All Rights for LAST FRONTIER Administered Worldwide by KOBALT SONGS MUSIC PUBLISHING
All Rights Reserved   Used by Permission

KINGS & QUEENS

TROMBONE

Words and Music by DESMOND CHILD,
AMANDA KOCI, BRETT McLAUGHLIN,
HENRY WALTER, MADISON LOVE,
HILLARY BERNSTEIN, JAKOB ERIXSON,
MIMOZA BLINSON and NADIR KHAYAT

Copyright © 2020 UNIVERSAL - POLYGRAM INTERNATIONAL PUBLISHING, INC., WARNER GEO MET RIC MUSIC, MAX CUT PUBLISHING,
ARTIST PUBLISHING GROUP, EMI APRIL MUSIC INC., BOB OCHOA'S HOMEMADE SALSA, KMR MUSIC ROYALTIES II SCSP,
PRESCRIPTION SONGS, CIRKUT BREAKER LLC, LIVEMADLOVE, ARTIST PUBLISHING GROUP WEST, BUDDE ZWEI EDITION, BUDDE MUSIC INC.,
JAKOB ERIXSON PUBLISHING DESIGNEE, KAYAT MUSIC, SONGS BY KAYAT, SONGS OF REACH MUSIC and H BOOM SONGS
All Rights for MAX CUT PUBLISHING and ARTIST PUBLISHING GROUP Administered by WARNER GEO MET RIC MUSIC
All Rights for EMI APRIL MUSIC INC. and BOB OCHOA'S HOMEMADE SALSA Administered by
SONY MUSIC PUBLISHING LLC, 424 Church Street, Suite 1200, Nashville, TN 37219
All Rights for KMR MUSIC ROYALTIES II SCSP, PRESCRIPTION SONGS, CIRKUT BREAKER LLC, LIVEMADLOVE
and ARTIST PUBLISHING GROUP WEST Administered Worldwide by KOBALT SONGS MUSIC PUBLISHING
All Rights for BUDDE ZWEI EDITION and BUDDE MUSIC INC. Administered by DOWNTOWN DLJ SONGS
All Rights for JAKOB ERIXSON PUBLISHING DESIGNEE, KAYAT MUSIC and SONGS BY KAYAT Administered by ST MUSIC LLC
All Rights for H BOOM SONGS Administered by SONGS OF REACH MUSIC
All Rights Reserved   Used by Permission

SEÑORITA

TROMBONE

Words and Music by CAMILA CABELLO,
CHARLOTTE AITCHISON, JACK PATTERSON,
SHAWN MENDES, MAGNUS HØIBERG,
BENJAMIN LEVIN, ALI TAMPOSI
and ANDREW WOTMAN

Copyright © 2019 Maidmetal Limited, Milamoon Songs, Stellar Songs Ltd., EMI Music Publishing Ltd., Songs Of Universal, Inc., Mendes Music,
Infinite Stripes, Back Hair Music Publishing, Universal Music Works, Please Don't Forget To Pay Me Music, Reservoir 416 and Andrew Watt Music
All Rights on behalf of Maidmetal Limited, Milamoon Songs, Stellar Songs Ltd. and EMI Music Publishing Ltd.
Administered by Sony Music Publishing LLC, 424 Church Street, Suite 1200, Nashville, TN 37219
All Rights on behalf of Mendes Music, Infinite Stripes and Back Hair Music Publishing Administered by Songs Of Universal, Inc.
All Rights on behalf of Please Don't Forget To Pay Me Music Administered by Universal Music Works
All Rights on behalf of Reservoir 416 Administered Worldwide by Reservoir Media Management, Inc.
All Rights on behalf of Andrew Watt Music Administered Worldwide by Songs Of Kobalt Music Publishing
International Copyright Secured   All Rights Reserved

WILLOW

TROMBONE

Words and Music by TAYLOR SWIFT
and AARON DESSNER

Copyright © 2020 SONGS OF UNIVERSAL, INC., TASRM PUBLISHING, SONY MUSIC PUBLISHING LLC and INGRID STELLA MUSIC
All Rights for TASRM PUBLISHING Administered by SONGS OF UNIVERSAL, INC.
All Rights for SONY MUSIC PUBLISHING LLC and INGRID STELLA MUSIC Administered by
SONY MUSIC PUBLISHING LLC, 424 Church Street, Suite 1200, Nashville, TN 37219
All Rights Reserved   Used by Permission

WITHOUT YOU

TROMBONE

Words and Music by BLAKE SLATKIN,
OMER FEDI, BILLY WALSH
and CHARLTON HOWARD

Moderately, in 2

Copyright © 2020 SONGS OF UNIVERSAL, INC., BACK HAIR MUSIC PUBLISHING, TWO HANDS AND A BIT PUBLISHING,
ELECTRIC FEEL MUSIC, OMER FEDI MUSIC, UNIVERSAL MUSIC CORP., WMMW PUBLISHING and SONY MUSIC PUBLISHING LLC
All Rights for BACK HAIR MUSIC PUBLISHING, TWO HANDS AND A BIT PUBLISHING, ELECTRIC FEEL MUSIC
and OMER FEDI MUSIC Administered by SONGS OF UNIVERSAL, INC.
All Rights for WMMW PUBLISHING Administered by UNIVERSAL MUSIC CORP.
All Rights for SONY MUSIC PUBLISHING LLC Administered by SONY MUSIC PUBLISHING LLC, 424 Church Street, Suite 1200, Nashville, TN 37219
All Rights Reserved   Used by Permission

Your favorite songs are arranged just for solo instrumentalists with this outstanding series. Each book includes great full-accompaniment play-along audio so you can sound just like a pro! Check out **www.halleonard.com** to see all the titles available.

12 Hot Singles

Broken (lovelytheband) • Havana (Camila Cabello) • Heaven (Kane Brown) • High Hopes (Panic! At the Disco) • The Middle (Zedd, Maren Morris & Grey) • Natural (Imagine Dragons) • No Place like You (Backstreet Boys) • Shallow (Lady Gaga & Bradley Cooper) • Sucker (Jonas Brothers) • Sunflower (Post Malone & Swae Lee) • thank u, next (Ariana Grande) • Youngblood (5 Seconds of Summer).

___ 00298576	Flute	$14.99
___ 00298577	Clarinet	$14.99
___ 00298578	Alto Sax	$14.99
___ 00298579	Tenor Sax	$14.99
___ 00298580	Trumpet	$14.99
___ 00298581	Horn	$14.99
___ 00298582	Trombone	$14.99
___ 00298583	Violin	$14.99
___ 00298584	Viola	$14.99
___ 00298585	Cello	$14.99

12 Pop Hits

Believer • Can't Stop the Feeling • Despacito • It Ain't Me • Look What You Made Me Do • Million Reasons • Perfect • Send My Love (To Your New Lover) • Shape of You • Slow Hands • Too Good at Goodbyes • What About Us.

___ 00261790	Flute	$12.99
___ 00261791	Clarinet	$12.99
___ 00261792	Alto Sax	$12.99
___ 00261793	Tenor Sax	$12.99
___ 00261794	Trumpet	$12.99
___ 00261795	Horn	$12.99
___ 00261796	Trombone	$12.99
___ 00261797	Violin	$12.99
___ 00261798	Viola	$12.99
___ 00261799	Cello	$12.99

Classic Rock

Don't Fear the Reaper • Fortunate Son • Free Fallin' • Go Your Own Way • Jack and Diane • Money • Old Time Rock & Roll • Sweet Home Alabama • 25 or 6 to 4 • and more.

___ 00294356	Flute	$14.99
___ 00294357	Clarinet	$14.99
___ 00294358	Alto Sax	$14.99
___ 00294359	Tenor Sax	$14.99
___ 00294360	Trumpet	$14.99
___ 00294361	Horn	$14.99
___ 00294362	Trombone	$14.99
___ 00294363	Violin	$14.99
___ 00294364	Viola	$14.99
___ 00294365	Cello	$14.99

Contemporary Broadway

Defying Gravity (from Wicked) • Michael in the Bathroom (from Be More Chill) • My Shot (from Hamilton) • Seize the Day (from Newsies) • She Used to Be Mine (from Waitress) • Stupid with Love (from Mean Girls) • Waving Through a Window (from Dear Evan Hansen) • When I Grow Up (from Matilda) • and more.

___ 00298704	Flute	$14.99
___ 00298705	Clarinet	$14.99
___ 00298706	Alto Sax	$14.99
___ 00298707	Tenor Sax	$14.99
___ 00298708	Trumpet	$14.99
___ 00298709	Horn	$14.99
___ 00298710	Trombone	$14.99
___ 00298711	Violin	$14.99
___ 00298712	Viola	$14.99
___ 00298713	Cello	$14.99

Disney Movie Hits

Beauty and the Beast • Belle • Circle of Life • Cruella De Vil • Go the Distance • God Help the Outcasts • Hakuna Matata • If I Didn't Have You • Kiss the Girl • Prince Ali • When She Loved Me • A Whole New World.

___ 00841420	Flute	$12.99
___ 00841421	Clarinet	$12.99
___ 00841422	Alto Sax	$12.99
___ 00841423	Trumpet	$12.99
___ 00841424	French Horn	$12.99
___ 00841425	Trombone/Baritone	$12.99
___ 00841426	Violin	$12.99
___ 00841427	Viola	$12.99
___ 00841428	Cello	$12.99
___ 00841686	Tenor Sax	$12.99
___ 00841687	Oboe	$12.99

Disney Solos

Be Our Guest • Can You Feel the Love Tonight • Colors of the Wind • Friend like Me • Part of Your World • Under the Sea • You'll Be in My Heart • You've Got a Friend in Me • Zero to Hero • and more.

___ 00841404	Flute	$12.99
___ 00841405	Clarinet/Tenor Sax	$12.99
___ 00841406	Alto Sax	$12.99
___ 00841407	Horn	$12.99
___ 00841408	Trombone/Baritone	$12.99
___ 00841409	Trumpet	$12.99
___ 00841410	Violin	$12.99
___ 00841411	Viola	$12.99
___ 00841412	Cello	$12.99
___ 00841506	Oboe	$12.99
___ 00841553	Mallet Percussion	$12.99

Great Classical Themes

Blue Danube Waltz (Strauss) • Can Can (from Orpheus in the Underworld) (Offenbach) • Jesu, Joy of Man's Desiring (J.S. Bach) • Morning Mood (from Peer Gynt) (Grieg) • Ode to Joy (from Symphony No. 9) (Beethoven) • William Tell Overture (Rossini) • and more.

___ 00292727	Flute	$12.99
___ 00292728	Clarinet	$12.99
___ 00292729	Alto Sax	$12.99
___ 00292730	Tenor Sax	$12.99
___ 00292732	Trumpet	$12.99
___ 00292733	Horn	$12.99
___ 00292735	Trombone	$12.99
___ 00292736	Violin	$12.99
___ 00292737	Viola	$12.99
___ 00292738	Cello	$12.99

The Greatest Showman

Come Alive • From Now On • The Greatest Show • A Million Dreams • Never Enough • The Other Side • Rewrite the Stars • This Is Me • Tightrope.

___ 00277389	Flute	$14.99
___ 00277390	Clarinet	$14.99
___ 00277391	Alto Sax	$14.99
___ 00277392	Tenor Sax	$14.99
___ 00277393	Trumpet	$14.99
___ 00277394	Horn	$14.99
___ 00277395	Trombone	$14.99
___ 00277396	Violin	$14.99
___ 00277397	Viola	$14.99
___ 00277398	Cello	$14.99

Irish Favorites

Danny Boy • I Once Loved a Lass • The Little Beggarman • The Minstrel Boy • My Wild Irish Rose • The Wearing of the Green • and dozens more!

___ 00842489	Flute	$12.99
___ 00842490	Clarinet	$12.99
___ 00842491	Alto Sax	$12.99
___ 00842493	Trumpet	$12.99
___ 00842494	Horn	$12.99
___ 00842495	Trombone	$12.99
___ 00842496	Violin	$12.99
___ 00842497	Viola	$12.99
___ 00842498	Cello	$12.99

Simple Songs

All of Me • Evermore • Hallelujah • Happy • I Gotta Feeling • I'm Yours • Lava • Rolling in the Deep • Viva la Vida • You Raise Me Up • and more.

___ 00249081	Flute	$12.99
___ 00249082	Clarinet	$12.99
___ 00249083	Alto Sax	$12.99
___ 00249084	Tenor Sax	$12.99
___ 00249086	Trumpet	$12.99
___ 00249087	Horn	$12.99
___ 00249089	Trombone	$12.99
___ 00249090	Violin	$12.99
___ 00249091	Viola	$12.99
___ 00249092	Cello	$12.99
___ 00249093	Oboe	$12.99
___ 00249094	Keyboard Percussion	$12.99

Stadium Rock

Crazy Train • Don't Stop Believin' • Eye of the Tiger • Havana • Seven Nation Army • Sweet Caroline • We Are the Champions • and more.

___ 00323880	Flute	$14.99
___ 00323881	Clarinet	$14.99
___ 00323882	Alto Sax	$14.99
___ 00323883	Tenor Sax	$14.99
___ 00323884	Trumpet	$14.99
___ 00323885	Horn	$14.99
___ 00323886	Trombone	$14.99
___ 00323887	Violin	$14.99
___ 00323888	Viola	$14.99
___ 00323889	Cello	$14.99

Video Game Music

Angry Birds • Assassin's Creed III • Assassin's Creed Revelations • Battlefield 1942 • Civilization IV (Baba Yetu) • Deltarune (Don't Forget) • Elder Scrolls IV & V • Fallout® 4 • Final Fantasy VII • Full Metal Alchemist (Bratja) (Brothers) • IL-2 Sturmovik: Birds of Prey • Splinter Cell: Conviction • Undertale (Megalovania).

___ 00283877	Flute	$12.99
___ 00283878	Clarinet	$12.99
___ 00283879	Alto Sax	$12.99
___ 00283880	Tenor Sax	$12.99
___ 00283882	Trumpet	$12.99
___ 00283883	Horn	$12.99
___ 00283884	Trombone	$12.99
___ 00283885	Violin	$12.99
___ 00283886	Viola	$12.99
___ 00283887	Cello	$12.99

Prices, contents, and availability subject to change without notice.
Disney characters and Artwork ™ & © 2020 Disney

Hal•Leonard®